The Power of Healing:
A Memoir of Loss & Victory

Simbi M. Animashaun

Dedication

Children are a gift from the Lord, a reward from a mother's womb. ~Psalms 127:3

I dedicate this book to my three beautiful children. They have given me the strength, courage, and inspiration to wake up each day and go hard for whatever I desire. Since becoming their mother, I have become a better woman. The daily love and admiration they show me, has given me the determination I need to write this book. I hope when they get older, they read this book, and it inspires them to live a fulfilling life too.

Children, one day, you will understand the sacrifices I made to provide a better life for you. I hope and pray that you all will grow up to love, protect, honor, and encourage yourself, me, and each other. I hope that you will love others, even if they do not love you. Please, do not be consumed with worldly possessions, but be consumed with your blessings, which are your gifts from God. If you always love and respect yourself first, you will never have to worry about anyone or anything trying to break

you. Last, but not least, lean on God (not your

own) for understanding. I LOVE YOU ALL SO

MUCH!!!!

Acknowledgment

First, I thank Jesus for his love, grace, and mercy. Without him, I would not be alive today to share my story with others. Despite all the sinful acts that I have committed, he has always repeatedly forgiven me. He has never given up on me, and he has always seen the best in me (even when I did not believe in myself). Thank you, God, for allowing me to write this book, *The Power of Healing: A Memoir of Loss &*

Victory, and for creating such a remarkable journey for me.

Additionally, I thank my family for loving me unconditionally and being there to support me whenever I needed them. I specifically thank my grandmother for always being there for me, through thick and thin. She taught me how to love and respect myself, no matter what situation I was in. She saw my God-given gifts early during my childhood, invested in my education, and pushed me to excel to my highest potential. As a result, I was the first person in

my immediate family to graduate college —
THREE TIMES!

Lastly, I thank my sisters, friends, professors, classmates, and colleagues who have heard my story, been inspired, and encouraged me to share it, by writing this book. Thank you for not being judgmental during the most difficult times of my life. Thank you for being there for me whenever I called, even after months and years had passed. Thank you for not giving up on our friendship and sisterhood.

7

Thank you for loving me when I did not love myself.

Forward

A Letter from My Grandmother

Dear Simbi,

Since you were a little girl, you have always been the "black sheep" in the family. I do not mean that in a bad way, but you always stood out from the rest of us. You were the first in our family to graduate college, and I am extremely grateful that I could witness and take part in your many successes.

Not only am I proud of this accomplishment, but I am also proud that you always stayed strong through your trials and tribulations. I am not certain whether I would have been able to survive some of the situations you went through (brain hemorrhage and pregnancy loss), but I instilled in you the power of prayer, and I am glad that you never gave up on God! I am glad you finally listened to Him.

Despite it all, at 80 years old, I get to watch you be an astonishing mother to your three beautiful children. A better mother than me. You have created a beautiful home filled with lots of love for them. My visits to your home are always pleasant; I always leave with a giant smile on my face. Your children are always happy! Again, I am very proud of you and all your accomplishments! You are a wonderful woman, mother, teacher, and granddaughter. I did not recognize how much you went through until I read your story. Thank you for sharing your story with me. I am inspired; hopefully, it will inspire others. God has kept you covered, and I am honored to be a part of your journey.

Keep pushing forward!

Sincerely,

Grandma

Table of Contents

Introduction

*O*n many occasions, reading a person's

story about their experience with traumatic

situations and the process they took to overcome

it, has brought me into a place of strength,

courage, and healing. I have spent countless

hours with God, sharing with him my vision for

this book. *The Power of Healing: A Memoir of*

Loss & Victory is intended to be a resource and

guide for those experiencing or have

experienced pregnancy and infant loss. I openly

share my personal experiences about my recurrent miscarriages and brain hemorrhage; how it affected my day-to-day routine; and my process of healing. I am also transparent about how my faith caused me to have a fulfilling life after the storm. My victory finally comes after recognizing that I needed to heal from all of life's challenges and embrace God's timing.

Many people do not understand how pregnancy and child loss can have a devastating effect on a woman's physical, mental, and emotional state unless they have personally experienced it themselves. After years of experiencing recurrent miscarriages, God finally answered my prayers. I became a mother. All three of my children are blessings from God, no matter how they were conceived, and I am thankful for each one of their precious lives. I will always ensure that they have the best life, better than I had, as much as possible.

Be reminded: Every person we meet has a story to tell and an opinion for you, but at the end of the day, you have to learn to put yourself first and do what is best for you. If not, these people will try to tell you "who you are," "what you should do," and "what you should be". That is not how we were created. God created us to all be uniquely designed and that is how we should live our lives every day. During my illnesses, I had people who showed no empathy or compassion towards me. I had people try to break my spirit. Shame me. Attack me. I barely had friends and family to call to check on my well-being. However, I used that time to strengthen and shape my faith. You will read my road to recovery and victory at the end of the book. I could not put every detail I wanted to in this book, but it will equip you with courage and inspiration. I hope it also gives you the knowledge you need to make wise decisions as it relates to your faith.

Unfortunately, I have had to deal with many traumas since a very early age; if only I could tell it all, but I have learned to use those situations as lessons to live life to the fullest. I was supposed to be dead, but I am here to tell my story! Life would be great if it came with a study guide, but since it does not, use my story (created with love) to achieve everything that

you doubt.

Chapter 1: Beginning of What Felt Like a Million Losses

I will walk by faith even when I cannot. ~2 Corinthians

*W*hen I was a little girl, I always played

"house" and pretended to be my dolly's mother. I enjoyed feeding them, changing their clothes, combing their hair, putting them to sleep (for naps and bedtime), and cuddling with them in my twin-sized bed. I am not sure why I was extremely fascinated with this kind of role-play, but it continued until I was about 14-15 years old. I was the only girl in my family, out of three children, raised in a single-parent household. My mother dated her long-time boyfriend throughout my childhood until he was sent to prison after trying to murder her. I never knew how a functioning, two-parent, and loving household looked, but as I got older, I knew I wanted to be a mother one day. I wanted to create a loving household filled with beautiful children. I wanted to raise my children in a functioning home.

After years of dating the wrong men, in April 2012, I finally met a man, Malachi, with whom I fell in love and planned on starting a family. Years before meeting him, I had graduated from college with a Master's degree in Middle Grades Education. I was working full-time as a middle school teacher for a public school system in Maryland. I was well-rounded and respected in my circle of friends. I routinely set goals and worked hard to achieve them. Every area of my life was going great.

I was also the President of The Ivy League Book Club and a certified Zumba instructor. I started attending the local church in my neighborhood every Sunday. I was not raised to attend church, but I desired a different journey for my life. I will be honest, I was not a saint nor did I live a perfect life. I sometimes partied on the weekends with my friends or with Malachi, but I always prayed to God for everything. Because of that, I believed God would bless me with whatever my heart desired at that time.

Throughout the first year of dating Malachi, we discussed having children regularly. We discussed it almost every day. I was ready to be a mother. His wife. I hoped that he was ready too. At least that is what he told me.

He always said, "The next woman I have a child with will be my wife."

I believed him, and I believed that woman would be me, but that dream was repeatedly shattered. In January 2014, I had my first miscarriage (at age 30), after dating Malachi for two years. Although we discussed having children regularly, we were not trying. Since we were dating long-distance, we wanted to be closer to each other, possibly in the same city, before we got married and started the baby-making process. He lived in Ohio. I lived in Atlanta.

Unexpectedly, I found out that I was pregnant on New Year's Day that same year. We were visiting each other every month, having unprotected sex, so I knew it would eventually happen. I just did not know when.

I remember the day I found out I was pregnant vividly. I had been feeling bloated and nauseous for a few weeks since Thanksgiving of the previous year. I did not think I was pregnant because honestly, I did not know what pregnancy felt like. But, I had missed my last period, and that never happened. My cycles were always regular. So, after returning home from partying all night at one of the hottest clubs in Atlanta for the holidays, I snuck to the bathroom to pee on the stick. Using the pregnancy test I bought from the pharmacy, days before, I was eager to discover if I was pregnant or not. While Malachi was sleeping, I tip-toed to the bathroom to take the pregnancy test. I preferred not to wake him up. He seemed exhausted.

If I am pregnant, then I will scream and
wake him. I want it to be a surprise.

After peeing on the stick, I waited patiently, excitedly, and nervously.

About 10 minutes later, I saw two blue lines appear on the stick. It was positive; I was pregnant! It was my first pregnancy, and I was very emotional as I read the results. As I mentioned earlier, I always wanted to be a mother.

I changed my mind about how I would share the good news with Malachi. He was still sleeping very peacefully in the bed, and I decided not to wake him.

With the pregnant stick still in my hand, I tip-toed back to my bedroom and placed the stick on the nightstand (do not judge me; it was dry by that time). I thought Malachi was asleep.

He turned around and whispered, "Honey, is everything alright?"

"I turned around to cuddle with you, and I did not feel you."

"Yes, I am fine," I responded. "I do have a surprise for you."

He turned over. Anxiously, I handed him the pregnancy stick. He held the pregnancy stick up in the air, saw the two blue lines, and smiled.

He said, "I already knew it. You have been very moody lately."

I shook my head. "I am so sorry!" I responded apologetically. "You never said anything."

Malachi replied, "I was not certain. I preferred not to scare you."

"I know we want children, but I do not believe we are not ready to be parents yet."

"We will talk about it more in the morning. Let's get some rest. I am exhausted."

He held me tightly in his arms and fell asleep. I could not sleep though; there were so many thoughts running through my mind.

Will I be a good mother? How should I break the good news to my family and friends?

Will it be a girl or boy? What should I name him or her? Will Malachi propose to me now? Should I move to Ohio?

The next day, we did not talk much about it. Instead, we planned a daytime date for the movies. I enjoyed spending time with Malachi; it was always so much fun. We were running late, as usual, so we quickly got dressed and jumped in the car. I believe we both wore sweatsuits, sneakers, and the biggest coat we owned because it was freezing outside. It had to be at least 26 degrees that day. When we stepped outside, the wind smacked us in the face. That is how cold it was. The movie theater was 5 minutes from my apartment, so it did not take us long to get there. He found the closest parking space to the movie theater. Because the wind was so disrespectful, we decided to race to the theater. Malachi won, of course. As he purchased our ticket, I went to the bathroom. I was cramping for some reason. I had to use the bathroom too. When I pulled my pants down, I was bleeding, but it was a light bleed.

OMG! Is this my period? Am I pregnant? But, the pregnancy test had two blue lines. This is confusing. I began to question if I was pregnant or not.

Hurriedly, I put on a thin maxi pad; I always kept them in my purse and pulled my pants back up. I did not think about it anymore. I did not even tell Malachi what I had just experienced. I just walked quickly back to the front entrance and met him at the ticket booth. I held his hand, we checked into our assigned theater, found seats at the top of the theater, and enjoyed the movie. I pretended as if nothing had happened. The movie, *Ride Along* (featuring Kevin Hart and Ice Cube), lasted for about two hours. We laughed the entire time, and I enjoyed each minute there with Malachi.

That night, we ate dinner and had sex. I had stopped bleeding. I checked before we did anything.

The next day, Malachi rushed to get to the airport, so he would not miss his flight back to Ohio. Still, we had not talked about the pregnancy. I wanted to know how he felt about it. My feelings remained the same; I was excited.

That next morning, I woke up excitedly to get ready for work. I did not share my good news with any of my colleagues yet. I did not share it with my family and friends either. I decided to wait, but I spent that entire day smiling and rubbing my stomach.

I am sure my students were wondering: *What the hell is wrong with her?*

I hardly smiled. Due to the disrespect I constantly experienced at that school, I had to be very strict with my students. If they were not scared, I am sure they would have blurted it out. They were that bold and assertive.

I continued the day with a giant smile on my face.

A few of my colleagues began to ask questions.

"Your man must have been in town? Why are you so happy?"

"Yes he was, and we had a wonderful time," I responded enthusiastically.

However, my world would turn upside down a week later. I experienced my first miscarriage. It was such a horrible experience.

On January 16, while standing in front of my class and giving directions to my students, I began to cramp terribly. On my way to work that morning, I had eaten a sausage biscuit and drank a cup of orange juice from McDonald's, so I did not think much about it. I thought it was gas, so I took a little Pepto-Bismol that was sitting on my desk, to relieve the pain and discomfort from the cramping. I wish I was prepared for what would happen next.

Being naive, I should have known something more serious was wrong. The night at the movie theater, I had been spotting. I continued to spot off and on for a few days after having sex with Malachi, but I ignored it. As much as I wish I could have prepared for this next experience, no woman can prepare for this.

As I sat on my stool, it began to feel like I was peeing on myself.

What is going on? I know I am not peeing on myself. What should I do? This is so embarrassing.

Moments later, I nervously looked down to the ground, and I noticed tiny droplets of blood were on my shoes. I stood up and noticed a small bloodstain on the stool. Luckily, I wore all black that day, so my students did not notice anything. They were working silently on their narrative essays. It was so quiet in the classroom that you could hear a thumbtack if I dropped it on the floor.

With my students focused on their assignment, I quickly ran out of my classroom to the nearest staff bathroom. I am sure they noticed that I had left the classroom because I could hear their voices, chattering, mid-way to the bathroom. I did not care.

When I pulled my pants down to see what was happening to me, my panties and pants were soaked in blood. I almost fainted, but in my mind, I knew that was a terrible idea. I felt it would be better not to cause a scene at work nor disrupt the learning environment. I quickly pulled my pants back up, ran out the front entrance of the school, into my car, and drove myself to Dekalb's nearest emergency room. I did not let any of my colleagues know what was happening at that moment, but on my way to the emergency room, I sent my Assistant Principal a brief text message to let him know that I had to leave due to an emergency. He understood and wished me well. Dr. Baker was always a supportive administrator.

By that time, I was starting to bleed heavily. I was releasing clots. I honestly did not know what it was at first; it just felt like I was peeing tiny raspberries. When I was finally admitted to a room, the nurses began to ask intake questions. I informed them that I was about 8 weeks pregnant. I think deep down, they knew what was happening, but they wanted to avoid saying anything at that time. I am sure they noticed the pathetic look on my face because the looks on their faces were blank. They showed very little emotion, and they hardly made eye contact with me. By that time, the cramps were getting worse, and now my pain level was at 10.

Still, the ER doctor (who was a fair-skinned man, maybe in his mid-30's), made me go through the unbarring experience of having a bloody ultrasound before informing me that I was having a miscarriage.

"I am sorry, ma'am," he said. "We do not hear nor see a heartbeat."

"You just had a miscarriage. Do you know what that is?"

I whispered, "No, not really."

Looking confused by my response, he began to hand me several fact sheets about miscarriages and explain the content to me. He showed little compassion as he read from the handouts. I did not expect him to, though.

He explained, "A miscarriage is the result of a failed pregnancy. It is often called a spontaneous abortion. Miscarriages usually occur before the 20th week because the fetus is not developing normally."

"Do you have any family or friends that can come here and support you? I know this news is difficult to digest alone."

"No, I do not," I responded with sadness. "I did not even tell anyone I was pregnant."

After we spoke about my miscarriage, he suggested that I have a dilation and curettage (D&C), which is a procedure performed to remove the dead fetus from inside your uterus after a miscarriage has happened. I agreed to have it done. This was the first medical procedure I had experienced in my life. It took them at least 10-15 minutes to perform the D&C, which was a horrifying experience. It felt like I was there for several hours as I lay on the hospital bed, waiting to be prepped for the procedure. I was so nervous; my hands were starting to shake. The doctor noticed my hands shaking and asked me if I needed help relaxing.

"I sure do!" I exclaimed.

So, he gave me a sedative pill to help me relax. Then, they gave me antibiotics, orally, to help prevent infections. He began to examine my cervix to determine if it was open and placed a speculum to keep it open. I could hear the speculum clicking as he inserted it into my vagina. Next, I began to hear a loud vacuum noise. I looked down and saw a long tube (attached to a suction device) being inserted, called suction curettage. The long tube would remove the contents of my uterus. It took about 5 minutes for him to scrape the lining of my uterus.

Finally, he removed a glob of tissue and placed it in a jar. He told me that the tissue would be sent to a pathology lab for testing. It looked awful, but at the same time, I felt bad looking at my dead baby in a jar. Once the bleeding stopped, the speculum was removed, and I was sent to the recovery room for an hour.

How did I feel? I was disappointed and in disbelief. I also felt lonely and unworthy. I was looking for someone to blame, but I ended up blaming myself. I was too embarrassed to call anyone or support; I did not even call Malachi.

What did I do wrong? This is my fault. What will Malachi think of me? Will he blame me for the loss of our child?

49

About an hour after being in the recovery room, I was discharged. I drove myself home, in pain (emotionally, mentally, and physically).

I could not take a shower yet, so I washed myself up and laid in bed thinking.

Why me, Lord? What did I do to deserve this? Why did you take my baby from me?

That night, I began to question my ability as a woman. I began to question God. I became angry and just cried myself to sleep. Thinking back, I had not had the chance to tell anyone (family nor friends) that I was pregnant. I felt embarrassed to call anyone now and tell them that I just had a miscarriage. I wish I had at least told my grandmother. I needed her support now, but no one knew, except for Malachi.

Around midnight, I woke up and called Malachi to share the devastating news with him.

"I lost the baby today," I murmured.

"What do you mean?" he questioned.

I responded, "I had a miscarriage. Can we talk about it later? I am drained and sore from the procedure I had today."

He whispered, "I am sorry, love. Do you need me to fly to Atlanta to be with you?"

"No, I will be fine," I said.

I was not fine. I was embarrassed to face him. I thought losing the baby was my fault. The next morning, I did not feel well, so I decided to stay home from work. My body was extremely sore. I was light-headed. I was also nauseous. I could barely get out of bed to walk to the bathroom. Luckily, I had a little strength to walk to the living room, so that is what I did.

I just laid on the couch for the entire weekend, unable to process what just happened to me.

I thought my current symptoms were the result of the D&C procedure I had just had, but months later, I would learn that I had just gone through an unexpected near-death experience.

What happened to my faith? Why am I questioning you, God?

I wish I had not questioned God. Now, I believe everything happens for a reason, and I believe at that time, God was not ready for me to experience the journey of motherhood. I would have been taking care of a baby by myself. Being a single mother, at that time, would have been too much for me to handle. I did not truly understand the roles and responsibilities of a parent, but now I do. I was not maturely ready for the responsibilities of a baby. Quickly, I learned to walk by faith.

Chapter 2: The Unexpected

*Come now, you who say, "Today or tomorrow
we will go into such and such a town and spend
a year there and trade and make a profit"— yet
you do not know what tomorrow will bring.
What is your life? For you, are a mist that
appears for a little time and then vanishes.*
~James 4:13-14

Six months after my first miscarriage, I would begin a new life in Ohio with Malachi. He felt bad for not being able to be by my side to support me during my miscarriage, so we decided that I would move in with him. We would both be able to save money too; that was our primary goal. In July 2014, after selling all the furniture in my apartment, I packed all my belongings, and Malachi and I drove to Ohio. It was about a 12-hour drive. We split the drive. He drove the first six hours while I slept. And then we switched. When it was my time to drive, Malachi had fallen asleep immediately after we switched positions. I turned some R&B music on really low and began thinking. My heart was pounding, and my thoughts were all over the place.

What am I doing? Am I making the right decision? I have never lived with a man before, will this work?

For the next three hours, I began wondering if I was making the right decision. I had not prayed about this move to Ohio. Malachi presented the idea to me one day and I just agreed to it. I ignored my feelings of uncertainty and turned the music a little louder. I looked over at Malachi; he was still sleeping peacefully. I smiled and continued to drive.

As days passed, I was instantly offered a teaching position at a charter school in Cleveland. I accepted. I even applied for graduate school. My major was Educational Leadership. I wanted to be a Principal one day. My professional life was quickly falling into place, but I was having a difficult time adjusting to my new city. My new home. My new family.

The city was small. The skies were always gloomy and cloudy. The air smelled bland. The trees and grass were all dead. There was no sign of life, and I was starting to become homesick. I tried my hardest to fit into my new environment. I tried extremely hard to be happy.

The next few months would be trial and error, but then the unexpected happened on the night of November 14th. This was the last class that semester, and for our final exam, we had to present a PowerPoint Presentation about all the important leadership strategies and tools we had learned during the eight-week session.

I was supposed to be graduating with a Master's degree in Educational Leadership the following year since the graduate program accepted transfer credits from a previous college I had attended in Maryland. I believe I was next in line to present. As I waited to present, I bit into a red velvet cupcake (my favorite flavor) to relieve some of the anxiety I had for presenting in front of a group of people. All of a sudden, I started to get a headache. This was not a regular headache; it was the "worst" headache I had ever had in my life.

One of my classmates noticed that I was in pain (I am assuming by the frown on my face) and asked, "Simbi, are you okay? You do not look too well."

I responded by telling her that I had a terrible headache, so she offered to give me aspirin to relieve the pain. I gratefully accepted. Unfortunately, it did not help. I still had a severe headache minutes later. Immediately, I informed my professor of my current physical state and asked to be excused to the bathroom.

On my way to the bathroom, I started to experience other challenges. I was having difficulty walking. I almost fell multiple times on my way to the bathroom. I had trouble speaking. I tried to call Malachi, but I could not press the buttons on my phone. There was numbness on the left side of my body. My vision was blurred. I could not see.

"What the hell is going on?" I mumbled to myself. "I'm too young for this!"

I had just turned 31 years old on October 2nd. I could not figure out what was happening to me. I was still young, and I did not have any underlying health concerns. I had only experienced the miscarriage earlier that year, so I was perplexed about my current state.

I had no idea what was happening to me nor how my life was about to change. Confused, I just stood in the bathroom stall. After about 15 minutes of being in the restroom, another one of my classmates, Mary, entered the restroom to check on me. I could not see her. All I could hear was her loud, stern voice.

"Simbi!" Mary shouted. "Where are you? What is up with you?"

I began to explain, as much as I could, all the symptoms I was experiencing. In a crackling voice, I mumbled,

"I have a terrible headache, and I cannot see. I am also having trouble talking to you now."

She insisted, "Girl, you do not sound too good. We need to get you to the nearest emergency room."

"Let me call an ambulance for you. I promise I will stay with you. I know you do not have family here."

"Think about it," Mary continued.

She then entered my stall and helped me walk to one of the lounge chairs in the hallway so that I could decide if I wanted to call an ambulance or not. Honestly, I wanted to avoid riding in an ambulance, so I passed her my cell phone (from my back pant's pocket) and told her to call Malachi. When he picked up the phone, Mary calmly began to explain to him what was going on with me. I could hear the worry in his voice as he asked questions about my current state.

He rushed to Cleveland (about a 25-minute drive) to take me to the emergency room. I closed my eyes, as I sat in the lounge chair, waiting for his arrival. It seemed like he was standing over me within 5 minutes. When he walked up to us, I could not see him, but I could

hear him and smell the fumes from his cologne.
He always smelled good!

"Honey?"

"What is going on?"

"I do not know," I pleaded, "Please, just take me to the hospital."

He gently grabbed me, my personal belongings, and helped me walk to the car. I struggled. He had to pick me up and carry me to the car. Luckily, he parked near the building. I was a solid 175 pounds (79.38 kg), so I am sure he struggled to carry me to the car. But, he never said a word. He never complained.

Within the next 10 minutes, we arrived at the emergency room, with high hopes of identifying the cause of the problem. After struggling to complete the intake forms, I was immediately placed in a room to be seen by the doctors. I remember being asked several intake questions and being unable to respond clearly.

The doctor asked, "Why are you here this evening? How are you feeling? What symptoms are you experiencing?

"I have a terrible headache!" I shouted.

He continued, "How long have you had a headache? When was your last period? Are you pregnant?"

Why is he asking if I am pregnant?

I felt like an infant who had just learned how to babble, and unable to effectively communicate my wants and needs. I was embarrassed but scared at the same time. I did not know how to feel, so I became emotionless.

They started to draw blood and asked for a urine sample. I am not completely sure what they were testing at that time, but 30 minutes later, the doctor and nurses returned to my room and informed me that I was PREGNANT.

"Pregnant?" I questioned.

It was a strong possibility that I could be. After I moved to Ohio, Malachi and I continued to have unprotected sex. But, I was not trying to get pregnant yet. Truth be told, I was still suffering emotionally from my first miscarriage earlier that year. I thought about it constantly. I was perplexed about the news I was being told.

"Is this happening?" I asked myself.

While questioning my pregnancy, the nurse returned to my room with a smile on her face and let me know further "good" news (so she thought). I was being discharged under the circumstances that I was pregnant. However, I had never heard or read of any woman experiencing the symptoms I had as a result of pregnancy.

My discharge did not sit well with me. Nothing seemed right. As Malachi pushed me out of the emergency room in a wheelchair, I began to vomit profusely everywhere. He managed to get me in the car quickly. Then, he tilted my head out of the passenger window for me to get some fresh air. I still felt extremely sick. During that 25-minute drive back home, I was miserable.

Over the next week, while at home, my symptoms worsened. I remained on bed rest. I still did not feel pregnant; although I vomited every chance I could get. I had Malachi contact my Principal to let him know I had a stomach virus, and I would be unable to return to work. I also had him email my college professors. I preferred not to fail my classes; I had been performing exceptionally well.

I know I probably was worried about the wrong things because I still could not walk, talk, see clearly, nor hold down any food. Any type of food Malachi brought me to eat smelled disgusting. One evening, he even brought me my favorite pasta dish from Olive Garden, which was the Chicken Parmigiana, a Caesar salad, and the buttery breadsticks. When I tried to eat it, it came right back up.

Malachi spent countless hours making sure I was comfortable and attended to. He fed me. He cleaned me. He helped me each day; even though he had other responsibilities to handle. For that, I will always be thankful for him. One night after being washed and put in the bed, I realized that your life can change instantly. The strong, independent, successful, and driven woman I was a year ago was now a woman who could not even take care of herself.

Five days later, I began to feel a bit better, so I set up an appointment with the nearest OB/GYN to check the status of the baby. Despite my current state, I was beginning to feel excited about being pregnant. When I arrived at the physician's office for my scheduled appointment, Dr. Bonk immediately noticed that Malachi had to help me walk into his office. He was a short, older man. He also wore a long white coat that covered the clothing he wore underneath. I could not even see his pants or shoes. That is how long his coat was. When he spoke, his voice had a strong African accent. Since I was also still unable to speak clearly, he started asking Malachi questions about my physical well-being.

He turned to Malachi, "How long has she been experiencing these symptoms? Can she eat food comfortably? How is her vision? I see that she keeps squinting her eyes a lot. Does she wear glasses or contacts?"

By the confused tone of his voice, it was very evident that something else was wrong with me. With little strength in me, I proceeded to share my story, particularly, what I had experienced that night of the incident and how I had been feeling over the last few days.

He continued, "Have you still been having headaches since being released from the emergency room? Which emergency room did you go to again? Did they perform any other tests besides a blood and urine test?"

Both Malachi and I tried to answer all of his questions with great detail.

He was extremely displeased that the doctors in the emergency room did not perform more tests. He then suggested that an ultrasound be performed to check the status of the baby. Still unable to see clearly, I lay on the bed, patiently waiting to hear the news.

He said, "There is not a heartbeat yet."

I began to cry. However, since I was only about 4-5 weeks pregnant, he determined it was too early to diagnose the pregnancy as a miscarriage. I am not sure how Malachi was feeling; he did not say anything. I tried to look over at him, for some sort of reaction, but his face was still blurry.

"Do not worry, Ms. Animashaun!" he responded. "It is still too early to hear a heartbeat. We will schedule another ultrasound in three weeks."

"Ok, thank you," I responded.

Even though I was ecstatic to hear that news, pregnancy was far from his concern, though. He was adamant that the symptoms that

I had experienced and currently experiencing did not correlate with pregnancy. As a result, he sent me to the local hospital for further studies.

Due to my inability to walk, I was transported in an ambulance to Mercy Hospital, about 5 miles (8.05 km) away from where I lived. I do not know the reason I had to ride in an ambulance. The experience was weird; I had never ridden in an ambulance before. My eyes were wide open the entire time, trying to see as much as I could. I was freezing inside the ambulance, so I was wrapped in warm blankets.

The dispatchers were two young, white males. They were very nice, attentive to my needs, and respectful.

Once I arrived at the hospital, I was immediately assigned to a room. The front desk attendant, an older black woman, already knew who I was.

"Welcome to Mercy Hospital, Ms. Animashaun," she politely said, "You are going to be staying with us for a few days."

"Do not worry! We are going to take good care of you."

At this point, I was tired of hearing, *do not worry!*

As soon as I entered my room, the doctors immediately started working: asking intake questions, drawing blood, taking urine samples, and measuring my blood pressure.

Here, we go again!

After the intake process was over, the doctors began to examine my body strength by conducting preliminary tests, which included hitting both of my knees with an instrument (it looked like a mini hammer). They noticed the weakness on the left side of my body. They also made me wiggle my fingers, one by one, which I had trouble doing.

Then, the doctors suggested that a magnetic resonance imaging (MRI) scan be conducted. Again, I was transported back to an ambulance, and taken to MetroHealth Hospital in Cleveland. No explanation was given; I was just transported. I was only told that this hospital specialized in neurology, which is the study of the nervous system. The nervous system is made of two parts: the central and peripheral nervous systems. It includes the brain and spinal cord.

I slept during this drive. I was exhausted by this time.

As soon as I was admitted to the hospital and assigned to my room, the new set of doctors immediately began performing their preliminary tests and also recommended that an MRI scan be conducted on my head. They explained the effect the MRI could have on the fetus, but I did not care. I signed the forms to have the MRI conducted. The procedure was excruciating. First, the noise was annoying. It was very loud! At that time, I was very sensitive to loud sounds. The tight space was also uncomfortable. I was always claustrophobic, and the word made more sense now. I could not wait until this was over, but the MRI procedure lasted one hour.

While waiting for my test results to return, I turned to look at the time on my phone. It was 10:30 PM. Due to the time, I ended up staying overnight at the hospital. That night, around midnight, one of the neurologists came to my room to finally share the results from my MRI scans. He scared me; I had just fallen into a deep sleep. He was an older white male, talked fast, but at the same, showed compassion for me. Before he started to share my test results, he reassured me that I would be fine. Then the phone rang, and he left quickly. I was confused.

What is going on here? What are my results?

Then, another doctor entered the room. His demeanor was quite different from the first doctor. He was a heavy-set, white male. He acted like he preferred not to be bothered. Very grumpy. As he introduced himself, he looked at the papers on his clipboard the entire time.

"I have some good and bad news," he said.

My life was about to change forever. The doctor informed me that there were two blotches of blood on my brain. In other words, I had a brain hemorrhage (bleeding on the brain) that night in class. Almost a week ago. That was the bad news.

The doctors said the good news was that it was a miracle that I was still alive. I could have died from the brain hemorrhage, but I was a survivor.

I had been laying in the bed, after unknowingly suffering a brain hemorrhage. After hearing this news, I was filled with a mixture of emotions. I was relieved, scared, nervous, disappointed, and devastated.

Due to the severity of the condition, a mental health therapist (she looked pretty young) entered my room to check on my mental well-being. I did not feel like being bothered after the news I had just received. I was still trying to process what happened to me. As she started to ask how I was feeling, her voice began to fade. I was done answering any more questions. Noticing my attitude, she tried to share some encouraging words with me, but nothing she said could make me feel better.

Womp, Womp, Womp!

The thought of dying was unbelievable. I remember laying on my side just daydreaming, wishing this was not happening to me. I was there alone, unable to talk, so it was hard for me to contact family and friends to let them know what was happening to me.

I also remember wondering what Malachi was doing. He had left the hospital almost 12-hours ago, and I had not heard from him. Bored, I decided to log onto Facebook. I spent a few minutes scrolling through my friend's pictures. Smiling at pictures of their beautiful children. Then, I decided to visit Malachi's page to see if he had posted anything. He had not posted anything, but his ex-girlfriend had tagged him in a video. Angrily, I watched a video of

Malachi out at a Micheal Jackson concert with his two sons and ex-girlfriend's two children. All I could do was shake my head. He was supposed to be at the hospital with me.

He eventually showed up, hours later. I do not remember the time. I just know I was very upset. Malachi and the doctor walked into my room at the same time. I was in a daze; the doctor had to shake me a little to get my attention.

.

The doctor had returned with more devastating news. He began to share my MRI results with Malachi.

The doctor explained, "Well, we noticed an old blotch of blood on your brain, which means that you had a previous brain hemorrhage. We need you to stay a few more days here. We need to run more tests. Are you pregnant?"

"Okay," I responded nervously. "Yes, I am."

I ended up staying in the hospital for about 3 more days to undergo several more tests. Initially, when the doctors asked me if I remembered ever being previously sick, I could not remember much. But, I beat myself until I remembered that after I had a miscarriage in January, I did become extremely sick after being discharged from the hospital. It all made sense now. I had suffered my first brain hemorrhage after my first miscarriage. WOW!

Chapter 3: The Painful Diagnosis

I am always with you. ~Matthew 28:20

*T*hat night, I called my family to let them know that I had just had a brain hemorrhage. I hated calling family with bad news. I disliked receiving it. Ten years before my incident, we found out that my oldest brother was murdered. He was shot several times, outside his home. His death broke my family, so I felt it would be better not to put my family through any more trauma, especially since I was so far away from home. So, I told Malachi that our conversation with my family would be brief.

I dreaded calling them that night because when I moved to Ohio, they were extremely upset. They did not agree with my decision to move in with Malachi, but I did not care. I thought I had it all figured out. I was in love with him. I was expecting and planning a bright future filled with love, a successful career, and prestige education. Unfortunately, all my expectations ended as failures.

The phone rang three times and my grandmother answered the phone.

In a shaky tone, "Hey, Granny! I am in the hospital. I have some bad news."

"I had a brain hemorrhage while in class a few weeks ago. The doctors are running some tests now."

I was having such a hard time trying to explain my condition to them, so I gave the phone to Malachi for him to finish the conversation. I could hear my mother screaming through the phone. I just laid down and turned my back towards the wall. I still could not talk clearly, so I knew they were having a hard time hearing me in such an unusual manner. As he began to explain, I tapped his shoulder.

I whispered, "Please do not tell them that I am pregnant."

I felt it was far too much information to explain to them at the moment.

The conversation did not end well. I heard more screaming. Cursing. I eventually took the phone back and told them that I would call them back as soon as the doctor provided additional information. I was exhausted. I fell asleep moments later.

The next day, I woke up to Malachi being gone. I am assuming he left after I fell asleep and visiting hours ended. As soon as I woke up, I was transferred to the Intensive Care Unit (ICU) floor to be monitored very closely. The nurses were very kind. There were so many; I really cannot remember specific names or faces. Every three hours, they were drawing blood, checking my blood pressure and heart rate, and giving me a dose of Ibuprofen for my slight headache.

During my three-day stay in the ICU, I found some time to email my professor to let him know what had happened to me during his class. I was worried about my grade in the class. I preferred not to fail, and I anticipated returning to finish my graduate program. But, that never happened.

We emailed back and forth that day, and he asked if I wanted any visitors.

I happily said, "Yes."

I had also received a text message from a friend who I had met at my school's training program. Her name was Christina. The next day, both Mr. Harper and Christina came to visit me in the hospital. I was so excited to have visitors. They brought flowers and lots of hugs. They stayed for about 30 minutes because visiting hours in the ICU were ending very soon.

During the next two days, I learned more about my illness. I was diagnosed with an arteriovenous malfunction (AVM). It is similar to a stroke. According to American Stroke Association (2019), "Normally, arteries carry blood containing oxygen from the heart to the brain, and veins carry blood with less oxygen away from the brain and back to the heart. When an AVM occurs, a tangle of blood vessels in the brain bypasses normal brain tissue and directly diverts blood from the arteries to the veins."

It is a severe condition. As a result of it, I could have been disabled (loss of muscle function throughout my body). I could have died. I laid in bed, just thinking.

What if I had died? Will I be missed? Will I be able to walk again? Will the baby survive? Will I be able to ever work? Take care of me again? Take care of a baby?

I did not know what my future would hold after my incident. I was petrified. I then began to question whether Malachi would leave me. Ever since I had moved to Ohio, he had become extremely distant. We hardly talked or spent time together. He would stay out all times of the night. We would argue about that all the time. I wondered if he was cheating on me. I needed to stop thinking about that; it was giving me a headache. So, I redirected my focus to my health. I picked up my cell phone and googled AVM. I needed to learn more about my diagnosis.

While researching, I learned that many women and men are born with an AVM and are unaware of it. I had been unknowingly living with an AVM for thirty years. I still did not know how the baby was doing. Unfortunately, its well-being was still not vital.

The next morning, the doctors scheduled another MRI to check the status of the AVM. When the results came back, there were no significant changes in the AVM, so the good news was that I could go home. I was so excited. I immediately called Malachi.

When he picked up the phone, I screamed with excitement, "I am being discharged from the hospital! I am coming home."

I asked, "Can you come to get me now?"

"I am on the way," he responded excitedly.

Surprisingly, I could not wait to go home. Malachi was there within 20 minutes. The nurse had already packed all my belongings, so when he arrived, she grabbed my bag, helped me get into a wheelchair, and pushed me into the elevator.

"Can I press the button?" I asked.

"Sure," she responded.

Struggling, I pushed the button to the first floor, but I did not care. I felt like a warrior who had just defeated his opponent.

When the elevator doors opened, Malachi stood there with an enormous smile on his face and a bouquet of red roses. We were both happy to see each other. He gently hugged me and kissed me on the forehead. That hug and kiss felt good. I had not received any physical affection since being admitted into the hospital. He put my bag in the trunk and helped me get into the car.

During the drive home, I sat in silence. Although I was happy to be discharged from the hospital, I still felt scared and nervous. I was living in Ohio with Malachi, far away from my family. I wish they were by my side during my road to recovery.

Who would take care of me?

One thing about my family is that when someone was sick or in need of help, we could always depend on each other.

Over the next few days, I would truly appreciate the value of family. Part of the reason

I had moved to Ohio was to get away from my family, but now, I wish my family was present. I wish they were in my hospital room every day to encourage me, protect me, and reassure me that everything would be fine. I had no other visitors, besides Malachi, my friend, and professor, while I was in the hospital those three days. It was such a depressing time.

I know that if I was in Atlanta, my family would have been by my side the entire time, especially my grandmother. She was always by my side; always present to support me. I began to reminisce about her. She had attended all my award ceremonies, graduations, auditions, and plays when I had performances, football games to watch me perform on the drill team, and even drove me to college on my first day. She paid for me to get driving lessons and purchased my first car. Not having her or other family members by my side was difficult.

Unfortunately, after being discharged from the hospital, I was still suffering from symptoms. I still could not walk, without support. I could barely formulate my words, let alone any sentences. The left side of my body was still numb. I could not wiggle or move my fingers or toes on the left side. I occasionally had headaches. The only medication that I was prescribed to relieve the headaches was Ibuprofen. It did help, though.

The next week, I had to return to MetroHealth Hospital for a scheduled angiogram and to have an ultrasound of the baby. Malachi dropped me off at the hospital. I did not want him to stay because the nurse had already told me to plan to be there all day. I knew Malachi would be unable to stay with me all day. He was a busy man.

First, I prepared for an ultrasound. When the sonographer walked in to conduct the ultrasound of the baby, the energy shifted in the room. I was experiencing low vibrations, and I quickly began to feel nervous. I had a feeling I was about to receive some bad news. The next 5 minutes, I received the bad news.

I found out that the baby indeed had no heartbeat.

"No, heartbeat. I am sorry, ma'am!" the sonographer murmured.

To hear those words again was extremely painful. During the ultrasound, the sonographer never turned the screen around for me to see the baby, so I already knew what that meant.

I had another miscarriage.

Quickly, I was forced to decide whether I wanted to have another D&C in the next 5 minutes. Or I could take a pill that would release the fetus while I was at home. Desperately and eagerly to go back home and crawl in my bed, I chose to take the pill.

Misoprostol, which allows the cervix to open and cause the uterus to cramp, so the pregnancy will pass, is the gigantic pill I was prescribed that day. It sounds excruciating, but I was tired of lying on the hospital bed and having all these procedures done on me.

I will take the pill tonight or in the morning. I am so tired of this! What is wrong with me?

That same day, I had to have an angiogram. This procedure took at least an hour. The preparation time was 30 minutes. The nurses shaved my private area and a long catheter was inserted in my groin area to my brain.

An angiogram is a sophisticated form of an MRI. X-rays were used to take detailed pictures of the blood vessels in my brain. Dye (a contrast agent) was delivered into the arteries making them visible on the x-ray. I was numb, so I did not feel anything, but I could see everything. It was cold in my room, though. I could feel that. The lights were dim. I felt like the room was spinning; it felt like a dream.

Is this real? Was this happening to me?

When the doctor entered the room, I just closed my eyes and kept them closed during the entire process.

When I finally opened them, I saw bright lights flashing, which was the camera taking images of my brain. That lasted another 15 minutes, so I closed my eyes back until the doctor told me the procedure was done.

"We are done, ma'am," he proceeded. "You may get dressed now."

116

I did not say anything. When he left the room, I rose and quickly put my clothes back on — feeling ashamed. I felt ashamed because I had another miscarriage, and the doctors were unable to provide any reasons why. I was starting to become worried that I would never be able to carry my children and be a mother. I began to lose faith again.

I called Malachi to pick me up from the hospital. He did. During our drive home, it was silent again (that was starting to be the norm). I was extremely hurt and devastated to even share with him the news about the miscarriage. I did not tell him until that night.

"Can we talk, later?" I asked. "I am exhausted."

"Yes, honey," he responded. "Is there anything that I can do to help you feel better?"

"No," I calmly said. "I just want to lay down."

When we arrived home, he helped me out of the car, into the house, up the stairs, and into bed.

Around 9:00 PM, I decided to take the abortion pill.

"Malachi," I yelled. "I need you."

I explained, "Today, during my ultrasound, the baby did not have a heartbeat. They gave me two options to release the fetus: either have a D&C, which is a surgical procedure or take an abortion pill. I did not feel like undergoing another procedure. So, I am going to take the abortion pill in a few minutes."

"I am sorry, Simbi," he stuttered. "Why did you not say anything earlier?"

"Do you need my help?"

"No, I want to do it alone," I responded. "I was overwhelmed earlier."

"I understand my love."

He hugged and kissed me. Then, he walked back downstairs. I walked to the bathroom. I sat in the restroom and placed the Misoprostol pill under my tongue. It felt like déjà vu. I felt like I had lived through this situation before.

Per the instructions, I had to lay down until I started cramping. So, I laid down in bed. Waiting. As I laid there, I started to think about my first miscarriage and how much pain I had experienced, both emotionally and physically. Having not one, but two miscarriages were emotionally draining.

About 20 minutes later, I started cramping. These were the worst cramps I had ever felt. It felt like someone was twisting my uterus into the form of a pretzel.

I ran to the restroom and released the pregnancy in the toilet. I could not even look down in the toilet. I immediately flushed the toilet, and I ran back to my bedroom.

For the next five days, I lay lifeless in bed. This was another norm now. My daily routine — laying in bed. Thanksgiving, which was one of my favorite holidays, was approaching. I believe the day was November 24, 2014. No matter where I was living, I always prepared or helped family and friends prepare a delicious feast. Every year, Thanksgiving dinner included:

turkey, candied yams, collard greens, green beans, dressing, corn casserole, potato salad, corn muffins. After dinner, there were always a variety of desserts to choose from. I loved my Aunt Elda's peach cobbler. When I lived in Maryland in 2008, she shared her peach cobbler recipe, and since then, I have cooked it every year for Thanksgiving.

Unfortunately, Malachi had to cook Thanksgiving dinner all by himself. Due to my condition, I was unable to help him cook in the kitchen nor did I get the opportunity to eat any of the food. All I could do was lay in bed. Thinking. That is all I could do. I was hurting. Physically. Emotionally.

I could hear Malachi downstairs, laughing and talking loudly, with his family. I wish I could join them, but I felt like shit! Learning my diagnosis was a hard pill to swallow. Having another miscarriage was even harder. Although I did not live a perfect life, I honestly tried to live a humble life. I could fathom why I was having such bad luck.

I had been baptized, but I had become extremely distracted in worldly possessions and love.

Was that the reason for my misfortunes?

After moving to Ohio, I barely read the Bible or attended church anymore. I had neglected my relationship with God, my family, and my friends while chasing love. Feeling devastated and alone that night, I decided to read the Bible. I will admit, it was a struggle. I started to get a headache after 10 minutes of reading. But, I began to feel better about my life.

Malachi left that night (not sure where he went) and stayed gone. In the middle of the night around 1:00 AM, I woke up and began to pray as loud as I could. I did not give a damn who heard me. I prayed for healing and thanked God for sparing my life. I needed to be thankful and show gratitude. I was not dead or crippled. I was still alive.

God, thank you so much for keeping me alive. You have been here with me during this journey every step of the way. You never

neglected me; instead, you have protected me!

Please heal me. I am ready to walk with you.

Chapter 4: Road to Recovery

The joy of the Lord is my strength. ~Nehemiah 8:10

*A*s I mentioned before when I was released

from the hospital, I still was experiencing

symptoms from the brain hemorrhage. I still had

to have help walking. I was embarrassed to use

a cane, so I relied on Malachi to assist me when

needed. I also could not effectively use my

hands anymore. I struggled to hold objects, such

as a cup or plate. My left hand was frail. During

my three-day stay in the ICU, several of the

doctors told me that I, physically, would never

be the same. But, my road to recovery was a

true sign from God, though. He always has the final word.

For three months, I faithfully went to physical and occupational therapy, to learn how to walk and use my arms again. I felt hopeless. I felt useless. I felt unloved. When I first arrived at the facility, I realized that I was not the only young person who was suffering from my condition. The facility smelled like old people; it smelled like mothballs and rubbing alcohol. I almost threw up when I first walked in. I was surprised, there were children, as young as five years old, in therapy too. My heart dropped, and I began to feel empathy. During my sessions, I could hear the children screaming. Crying. Kicking. Having tantrums. Physical therapy is extremely painful, especially in the beginning.

Before my physical therapist, a young woman who looked like she had just graduated from college, began to start training, we sat down and talked about the incident. She wanted me to share my feelings about it. We created 4-5 goals I wanted to accomplish during my time in therapy. They were:

1.Do not give up!

2.Become independent again.

3.Push myself to use my hands and legs
(without any support).

4.Finish my graduate program.

5.Become a mother.

After my personal goals were created, she
began to question my last goal. She wondered
why I chose to "become a mother". Then she
began to ask me about my life before the
incident. No one had ever asked me about my
prior life. I like the fact that she took the time to

get to know me personally. I informed her that I had just had a miscarriage the week before I started therapy.

At that moment, she stopped talking and hugged me. I had not been hugged or shown any affection, besides Malachi, since I became sick. I told her what the doctors said about me never being the same.

She responded by saying, "They are right. You will never be the same. You will be better."

I immediately smiled and was determined to get better! Therapy sure was difficult. I was still in pain, but I was determined to push myself, even with little encouragement. During my recovery process, I still had very few visitors. I had no additional help at home beside Malachi.

One day, a new thought clicked in my mind. Instead of feeling sorry for myself, I needed to be thankful and appreciate the life I still had. God allowed me to live. I was being given a second chance at life. Instead of using that testimony to be powerful; I was using it as a crutch to be negative and beat myself up about my illness.

I never hated God, but I still wondered and questioned: *Why me?*

But, when I changed my thinking, my situation started to change as well. Days later, my prayers were being answered.

Ring, ring, ring.

I answered, "Hey, Granny! How are you doing?"

"Hey Baby Girl, I am doing fine," she responded, "I am coming to see you!"

When she told me that, I did not ask any further questions.

I said, "Thank you, Granny! I cannot wait to see you."

The next week, my grandmother rode the Greyhound bus from Atlanta to Cleveland to help take care of me. I know for a fact that that bus trip took at least sixteen hours. That made me feel good. She was the only person in my family to visit me during my illness, and for that, I will forever be grateful for her love and support. Malachi's father, maternal grandmother, and aunt also came to visit me the next few days. They were the only ones in his family in Lorain to visit me during this time. But, it did not matter at this point. I prayed about it, the lack of support from family and friends, and leaned on God for his love, support, and encouragement. The people, including my neurosurgeon and physical therapist at the time, filled the void that I had from that lack of support from my family and friends.

As a result of that moment, I learned that *life is too short to worry about anything*.

While I was worrying, God was creating a road of recovery for me. At the end of my therapy sessions, which was March 2015, I was not 100% cured, but guess what, I could walk, see clearly, and speak independently. At the end of that month, my Family Medical Leave Act (FMLA) ended, and I had to return to work. Time had flown by, and I could not believe that my doctors were even releasing me to return to work. Before I could process what I had just experienced for the past twelve weeks, I was instantly surrounded by my seventh-grade students, at The Prep. They were excited to see me doing so well; they showed me so much love and compassion.

Chapter 5: On an Emotional Rollercoaster

Elijah was afraid and ran for his life... He came to a broom bush, sat down under it, and prayed that he might die. "I have had enough, Lord," he said. "Take my life; I am no better than my ancestors." Then he lay down under the bush and fell asleep. All at once an angel touched him and said, "Get up and eat." ~1 Kings 19:3-5

*H*appiness sure does not last long.

Just when my life was beginning to change, and I was close to living a normal life again, I received some devastating news. One day, Malachi decided to treat me to dinner. He told me that I had been through a lot, and he wanted to wine and dine me. I put on one of my new outfits that had been hanging in the closet since I moved to Ohio.

I had just gotten my hair done earlier that day. It was a sew-in bob with a bang. I wore a black fur jacket, a pair of fitted black jeans, a white long-sleeved shirt, and fur boots that matched my jacket. I applied some red lipstick to compliment my outfit. I was looking good. I was feeling great. I was finally getting out of the house to enjoy some alone time with Malachi.

We drove to Red Lobster. On our way there, Malachi kept looking down at his phone. I did not say anything to him about it.

I just thought to myself, *This dude is rude!*

But, I wanted to enjoy my first outing since my incident, so I decided not to say anything.

Dinner was wonderful. Unfortunately, I am allergic to shellfish, so I ordered the baked salmon, mashed potatoes, and creamed spinach. While eating dinner, we had a great time laughing and cracking jokes on funny-looking people who walked into the restaurant. I also ordered my first alcoholic beverage, and it sure did hit me hard. I was lit immediately.

Twenty minutes later, I was ready to go home. I was sleepy. My head was beginning to hurt. I probably should not have consumed any alcohol yet. I told Malachi how I was feeling, and he agreed we should go. Our waiter, a young black male, boxed our leftovers and asked if we wanted to order dessert.

"Not tonight," we both said at the same time.

Malachi paid for our bill and left the waiter a tip.

On our way home, Malachi started to continuously look down at his phone.

This time I said something.

I said, "What is going on honey? Why do you keep looking down at your phone? Is everything alright with you? Are you in danger?"

Moments later, my phone began to buzz. I was receiving a text message. And another text message. I quickly reached for my purse to grab my phone, not knowing what I was about to read.

I looked down at my phone and the message read: "Hi, this is Melissa. I thought I should let you know that I am five months pregnant with Malachi's baby."

Melissa was his ex-girlfriend, who he claimed was a horrible person growing up. I could not believe the news I was receiving. I looked over at Malachi; he said nothing. This was not the time for any more devastating news. I showed very little emotion; I did not know how to feel. Again. I had another emotional blockage. I just zoned out that night. I did not argue. I did not ask any questions. At that very moment, I did not care. When I got home, I just walked upstairs and laid in the bed. I hoped Malachi would not join me, and he did not. How was I supposed to feel? How was I supposed to react? I mean I had almost died 4 months earlier. I was still trying to deal with my illness and current state.

It took years for me to process the "baby" situation, but I have now given it to God. It was never my problem. It was never my worry. At the time, it was difficult to accept the baby or even be around him (after I decided to stay in the relationship) because of my misfortunes with having children. I never blamed the baby, but mentally, emotionally, and physically, I was still suffering from my recurrent miscarriages. I blamed Malachi for cheating on me. For hurting me at such a challenging time in my life.

My life had been a disaster since I moved to Ohio. I believe it was a sign from God, and it was time for me to listen. I felt like God was telling me to go home, back to Atlanta. I was listening, but barely! I recognized that nothing was going right for me, and I probably should not have moved there in the first place. But, I still barely listened because Malachi somehow convinced me to stay. He convinced me to stay with him. He promised me that things were over between him and Melissa. As angry and disappointed as I was in him, I stayed, not because of love, but because I was afraid.

After my brain hemorrhage, I was not confident in my ability to live on my own yet. I was barely thriving at work. Happily, the school year was ending in a week. It was June 2015. I will be honest, it was a struggle waking up each morning to get dressed to teach over a hundred kids. It was difficult remembering names. I could not tolerate so much noise (middle schoolers are noisy). I could not stop thinking about the latest bad news I had just received. That next week, I had a follow-up appointment with my new neurosurgeon, Dr. Gerrett, to determine the next steps in my recovery process. Based on the status of the AVM, I would either have to have open brain surgery, which could leave me like a vegetable, or have a non-invasive procedure called Gamma Knife

Radiosurgery (GKR). I became overwhelmed again.

Before a decision was made, I had to have another angiogram completed. I prayed that night. I called a prayer warrior, Pastor Regina, and she also prayed with me. The following week, I had the angiogram completed, and when the results returned, the AVM had healed. I did not need to have open brain surgery. GKR would be used to treat the malfunction. I met with the specialist at Cleveland Clinic, who would be performing the GKR, to see if I was a potential candidate. After our initial consultation, he determined that I was a candidate, but the procedure could not be performed if I was pregnant.

I had to schedule an appointment with my gynecologist the following week to take a pregnancy test. I was nervous.

What if I am pregnant? I cannot be. Maybe I am. I do not want to be. I am not ready.

So many thoughts were racing in my head. I walked into my assigned room the day of my appointment with sadness. The nurse led me to the scale.

"Ms. Animashaun, you weigh 180 pounds (81.65 kg)," she said.

I responded out loudly, "Yeah right, ma'am. Your scale is a lie!"

I was in denial that I weighed that much. My weight was always between 145-160 pounds. I gave a urine sample and proceeded to my room.

My gynecologist, a slim white male, quickly entered my room 5 minutes later and said, "You are pregnant! Congratulations!"

"Congratulations! This is not a good time for me to be pregnant. I was supposed to schedule the Gamma Knife Radiosurgery this month." I responded.

I almost fell off the table. The next day, I received a phone call from Cleveland Clinic letting me know that my GKR procedure was postponed.

Chapter 6: Questioning God Again

And we know that in all things God works for the good of those who love him, who have been called according to his purpose. ~Romans 8:28

Was I excited that I was pregnant again?

No, but I needed something spectacular to happen in my life after the storm; I had blocked out that Malachi's ex-girlfriend was also pregnant by him. I made sure I did everything right that I thought a pregnant woman should be doing: taking a daily prenatal vitamin, sleeping on my left side, eating fruits and vegetables, and avoiding eating certain foods and activities. The day came for me to have an ultrasound. I WAS NERVOUS!! I decided to go to my doctor's appointment alone again. I was still embarrassed.

During the ultrasound, it seemed like everything was happening in slow motion. The room began to spin as I lay on the bed to prepare for the ultrasound. When the sonographer entered the dark, she smiled and sat down to start the ultrasound. After placing the cold gel on my stomach, she began to slide the machine up and down my stomach. My eyes remained on the back of the screen; I waited for her to turn it around, so I could see the baby's heartbeat. She never turned the screen around. I already knew what that meant.

She quickly rose and said, "Ms. Animashaun, I am going to get the doctor. He will review the ultrasound with you."

When the doctor entered the room, "I am so sorry," he started to utter the most heartbreaking words, "Ms. Animashaun, there is no heartbeat."

I had suffered another miscarriage, which again left me devastated. This was my third miscarriage.

I started thinking to myself: *What are you (the doctor) sorry for? I do not want any sympathy. It is not your fault. I blame you, God. Why are you putting me through this repeated trauma? What did I do wrong in my life to deserve this?*

I then began to question my ability as a woman.

Am I a real woman? Will I ever be a mother?

I had been bashed and attacked by Malachi's ex-girlfriend about my inability to carry children, during one of our arguments. To this day, I am not sure why she harassed me or tried to hurt me by attacking my ailment. To be bashed for losing a child by a woman, a mother of four herself was very disturbing. I do not care how much I dislike a person, I would never bash someone for losing a child or even having an ailment. God dislikes ugly!

After this miscarriage, I felt I needed to focus on getting the AVM treated. I was ready to have the GKR procedure. I tried my hardest to bury the miscarriages and just forget about them. I was going to make sure I did not get pregnant again because I was damaging myself, in so many ways. The anticipation of the procedure was keeping me up at night. I called Cleveland Clinic the next day and rescheduled the procedure for the following month.

Unfortunately, when the time arrived for me to have the GKR procedure, I found out I was pregnant again. I fainted at this news. I was unhappy about being pregnant so soon. As much as I tried to mask my pain, I was still dealing with the devastating news of being cheated on. I did not want my first child to be born in a chaotic situation. I did not question God this time. I just prayed about it.

At my doctor's appointment for my first ultrasound, he whispered those devastating words again, "No heartbeat, Ms. Animashaun."

When I heard the news, I was relieved, but I still began to question God again.

Why do you keep allowing me to get pregnant and then lose the baby? Why do you keep doing this to me, God? Please tell me what

I did or am I doing wrong.

If I continued to get pregnant, I would not be able to have my procedure. I did not want to have another brain hemorrhage, so my doctor strongly encouraged me to get on birth control. I jumped at the idea. That same day, I received a Depo-Provera birth control shot.

In September 2015, I prepared to have the GKR procedure at Cleveland Clinic. My grandmother drove the Greyhound bus again to be there to support me during this process. I was so excited to see her! The dedicated love she has for me is the same love I want to have for my children. That night, we sat downstairs catching up on life. I did not tell her about Malachi's baby on the way, my recent pregnancy, and my miscarriage. I did tell her that I was questioning God about my sickness. She was not happy to hear that my relationship with God was starting to become weak.

She paused, and then the moment of truth began. I needed to hear this, and I listened quietly and patiently without saying a word.

She reflected, "It is that man! He is blinding you. He is changing you. You used to believe in God. You never questioned him and now you are. Occasionally we think we have found love, and honestly, that is not love approved by God. So, unfortunately, Simbi, I do not think Malachi is the right man for you. You all have two different agendas, and his agenda is fast-paced."

I did not know what that meant, but she continued, "I know you love him, but is love worth losing your life? Destroying your mind, body, and soul?"

The truth began to sink in.

Chapter 7: The Procedure

*Don't be afraid, for I am with you! Don't be
frightened, for I am your God! I strengthen
you–yes, I help you–yes, I uphold you with my
saving right hand! ~Isaiah 81:10*

The day of the procedure was the longest 8 hours ever! It took 30 minutes for me to check-in at the hospital, which included completing a stack of paperwork: questionnaires about my medical history, liability forms, financial obligation forms, and much more. I had never signed my name so many times in one day. This caused my anxiety levels to rise, but Malachi and my grandmother were there to cheer me on and reassure me that I was going to be fine.

Once I made it to the operating room, it seemed like I was laying on that hospital bed for days. The next steps in the preparation process made my skin crawl. Preparation included receiving numbing shots in four places on my scalp. As the surgeon began to explain the next steps, he drew two X's on my forehead using a black Sharpie. Then he attached two hair clips to the back of my head.

Why is this doctor marking two points on my forehead and two points in the back of my head? What the hell are they about to do to me?

"These four points that are being marked are where the helmet will be placed," he explained.

Helmet?

He continued, "Before we drill the pins in, which holds the helmet, I need to numb you."

The needles were so long; at least 3-4 inches long. When he was done, he quickly left the room. I sat there, in silence, until the numbing shots kicked in.

After about 10 minutes, I could not feel anything. I tried to pinch myself. Nothing.

Wiggle my toes. Nothing. Scratch my skin. Nothing. This was such a weird feeling.

The surgeon returned, poked me with a needle, and asked, "Did you feel that, Ms. Animashaun?"

Confusingly, I replied, "No, should I?"

He did not even say anything back, just shook his head. Next, he used a specialized device to drill four pins into the four places he marked, in my head. I am so happy I could not feel anything because the sight of the pins being drilled into my head was frightening. After the head frame (better word to use than helmet) was attached, they made me sit back in the lobby with Malachi and my grandmother. I was scared to leave the room; I did not want them to see me with that head frame drilled in my scalp. I can only imagine how they would be feeling and thinking. I walked out slowly, but with a (fake) smile on my face. When they saw me, they both said nothing. When I sat down in my seat, no one still said anything. We sat there in silence.

Then, I decided to crack a joke to break the silence.

I asked, 'Who do I remind you of?"

They both begin to laugh.

"Frankenstein," Grandma responded.

We all laughed again. Fifteen minutes later, it was time. Time for me to undergo the procedure.

The surgeon entered the waiting lobby and declared, "We are ready to begin your procedure, Ms. Animashaun."

Nervously, I stood up. Both Malachi and my grandmother kissed my hand and whispered,

"Do not worry! God has covered you already. You will be fine."

During the procedure, they slid me through the gamma knife radiosurgery machine. It was similar to an MRI machine. I closed my eyes and waited for it to be over. As my eyes were closed, I prayed that God would allow this procedure to be successful. The procedure lasted for an hour. I think I may have fallen asleep for about 45 minutes, which was normal for the majority of GKR patients. During the procedure, I did not feel anything nor did I hear any noise.

When it was over, the head frame was removed. Ouch! By that time, the numbing shots were wearing off. Having that head frame removed was excruciating. I could feel everything now. Immediately, I had the biggest headache, felt nauseous, and experienced bleeding at the pin sites.

Usually, after the procedure, patients are expected to wait at least an hour in the recovery room. But eager to leave the facility, I told the surgeon I felt fine. He began to discuss the discharge procedures. I respectfully interrupted and asked if Malachi and Grandma could join the discussion. The nurse grabbed them in less than five minutes, and the surgeon continued to discuss after-surgery care, my treatment plan, potential symptoms, and follow-up information.

He pleaded, "These are the potential side effects that you will experience after the procedure:

1. Nausea and vomiting
2. Tenderness where the pin sites were inserted.
3. Headaches.

4. There may be hair loss where the radiation was directed.

5. Dizziness.

6. Damage to surrounding areas in the brain."

He continued, "You should be able to resume normal activities within 1-2 days, but I recommend you take it easy for a few days. You have been through a lot these last six months. The pin sites should also heal on their own. You can remove the bandages tomorrow afternoon. If your symptoms get worse, please do not hesitate to call us. Lastly, you may resume bathing as usual."

Nervously, I asked, "What is the success rate of gamma knife radiosurgery?"

He responded, "In your case, the procedure should be 90% successful."

"Yes! Thank you for everything!" I declared.

During the drive home, I sat in silence reminiscing on life. I could not believe I just had to undergo a procedure that would save my life. Although life had taken a drastic turn, I was surviving! That very day, instead of losing hope and faith again, I became a prayer warrior. I prayed every morning, afternoon, evening, and night. I thanked God for my misfortunes and blessings. I thanked him for this test and this testimony.

Months later, I decided to move into my apartment. I was tired of the drama and the chaos with Malachi and his ex-girlfriend. She continued to harass me, by calling and sending me offensive text messages. I guess she wanted to make my life a living hell. I had had enough of it! I did not deserve any of this. I wanted peace. I wanted quiet. When I moved into my apartment, I was relieved. I bought all new furniture and decorations; I wanted to avoid seeing anything that would bring back any unwanted memories of my past.

One night as I sat in my bed alone, it had to be about 2:00 AM, God spoke to me. I immediately began to think about Atlanta. I began to miss home. My family and friends. I fell asleep and immediately began to dream about living back in Atlanta. And, that is what I did.

When I shared my good news with Malachi, of course, he was upset, but I did not care. He did not want me to leave. I could not understand the reason he wanted me to stay. I was unhappy, miserable, and tired of being mistreated. I was ready for something great to happen. In June 2016, I packed all my belongings up in a U-Haul truck, and my father helped me move back home to Atlanta. During that 12-hour drive, I continuously thanked God for sparing my life over and over again.

After moving back to Atlanta, my life would change for the better. I immediately found a place to live and accepted a teaching position back at my old school. I also researched and secured a reproductive specialist, therapist, and church home that I started to attend regularly. I started hanging out with my family and friends again. Things were falling into place. I was feeling good. I was happy; I was genuinely happy. I had not felt this way in such a long time.

One night as I sat in my apartment that night, I wondered:

Was it wrong for me to question God?

I felt awful for doing so, but I know God is forgiven. So, I started to pray and ask for his forgiveness. I also started to read the Bible. As I read the Bible, many believers questioning God. Questioning why evil things were happening to them, but they prayed faithfully, and God eventually answered their prayers.

In James 1:5-6, it says *if any of you lacks wisdom, let him ask God, who gives generously to all without reproach, and it will be given him. But let him ask in faith, with no doubting, for the one who doubts is like a wave of the sea that is driven and tossed by the wind.*

Oftentimes, we tend to question God with a rebellious and selfish heart; not wanting to know the truth. I did just that. I was unable to see the future, so it was hard for me to see the

184

brilliant plan God had in store for me. Now, I understand that everything does happen for a reason. Instead of questioning God, ask for wisdom and guidance. And expect and be prepared for an answer. It may not come when you want it to, but it will come at the right time. I give God thanks every day, and I always wait until he tells me to move.

Chapter 8: Journey to Motherhood

God blessed them and said to them, "Be fruitful and increase in number; fill the earth and subdue it. Rule over the fish in the sea and the birds in the sky and over every living creature that moves on the ground." ~Genesis 1:28

*A*fter I settled into my new home and job in Atlanta, I sought the reason I had had four miscarriages. It was important for me to understand because I believed there was still hope. I started my journey to motherhood in September 2016. I searched and searched for a reproductive specialist who would accept my medical insurance and was affordable. These facilities were very strict about the type of insurance they accepted; services were pretty expensive too! Finally, I found a few physicians, so I used the Internet to search for reviews and narrow down my list. That night I prayed about the process.

The next day, Dr. Margaret Sam, a fertility physician at Shady Grove Fertility Clinic stood out among them all. Her educational background and experience were impressive.

At my initial consultation, I walked nervously to the facility. When I completed all my intake forms, I was escorted to Dr. Sam's office. As soon as I walked in, I sat down in the seat in front of her desk and began to scan her office. It was very inviting, and it smelled of freshly picked red roses. On her wall, hung her degrees, certificates, pictures of babies, and holiday cards. I was not trying to be nosey and all in her business, but I looked closer and saw that they were cards and pictures of her previous or current patients. I am assuming they were patients who she helped become mothers. I continued to scan her wall. Out of curiosity, I decided to read a few cards, but then she walked with a big smile on her face.

Looking down at her chart, she asked, "Good Morning Ms. Animashaun. How are you feeling today?"

I responded with a smile. "I am doing well. Blessed. I do have a problem, and I pray that you can help me. Are you ready for me to share?"

I began to share my story, dating back to the past two years, explaining in great detail my experiences with having a brain hemorrhage and recurrent miscarriages.

After I finished sharing my story with her, she proclaimed, "Do not worry! We are going to figure this out. You are going to be a mother, no matter what it takes."

That smile on my face became bigger. She wanted me to come back for a follow-up appointment, so I scheduled an ultrasound and to have blood work drawn, for the following week.

Ugh! I hate ultrasounds, and I hate having my blood drawn.

At my next visit with Dr. Sam, she again greeted me with a smile on her face. She was always happy.

She was an older, fit, white woman. She was very passionate about her job, and I could tell she loved her patients. This appointment only took about thirty minutes. As she led me to the ultrasound room; my heart immediately began to race. I do not know the reason. I was not pregnant, but while getting undressed, all the memories of my past ultrasounds resurfaced. I started to feel sadness. Dr. Sam washed her hands, and then put on a fresh pair of plastic gloves. She picked up a tube of gel and proceeded to put it on my belly. This time, it was warm. In the past, it was always cold. As she examined the screen, she paused for a moment.

She asked, "Are you aware that you have about four fibroids? They are tiny"

I already knew that, so she proceeded to share additional information.

"You also have Polycystic Ovary Syndrome (PCOS)," she continued, "Do you know what PCOS is?"

"No, I never heard of it," I responded.

PCOS is a hormonal disorder causing enlarged ovaries with small cysts on the outer edges. My ovaries were not enlarged, but I had small cysts on the outer edges. Fortunately, I had never experienced any of the major symptoms, which is why she determined my case was mild. Women with PCOS symptoms usually experience heavy menstruation cycles,

194

obesity, hair loss, unwanted hair, infertility, acne, and depression. I was grateful to only have a mild case of PCOS.

When she concluded the ultrasound, I got dressed and went back to her office. There, we reviewed more information about PCOS. She then gave me a folder that had articles, information sheets, pamphlets, and other resources to help me learn more about PCOS. She proceeded to tell me that the cause of PCOS is unknown and there is no cure. PCOS affects thousands of women who are trying to get

pregnant, so I wondered if this was the cause of
my recurrent miscarriages.

At the end of the appointment, she explained
that she was placing me on a medication called
Metformin. It is used to prevent or treat
diabetes. Even though I did not have diabetes,
my sugar levels were extremely high. I learned
that high sugar levels can also affect conception
and can cause infertility. After the bad news, she
delivered some good news. By taking this
medication consistently, there was a strong
chance that I would not only get pregnant but

would also be able to carry my children successfully.

When I left the office, I picked up my medication from the nearest CVS Pharmacy and I immediately started taking the medication. I experienced the side effects, from taking the medication, right away. The side effects included extreme diarrhea, loss of appetite, and weight loss. The diarrhea was my least favorite side effect. I mean I was using the bathroom 5-6 times a day. No matter what I ate or had to drink, it was immediately released. Despite the effects of taking the medication, I began to feel good about myself. I began to feel beautiful. I had lost over five pounds within a month. I had more energy. I was looking good!

Dr. Sam also paired me with a nutritionist. We only spoke on the phone, but when she called, she always spoke in a low, pleasant voice. During our initial conversation, we discussed her role in my journey to motherhood, which was focusing on what I injected into my body. I began to learn that certain foods can negatively impact fertility in women with

PCOS. We created some nutritional goals, and she shared some suggestions for changing my diet. We scheduled a follow-up appointment for six weeks. By January 2017, I had lost over ten pounds, and I was the healthiest I had ever been.

I was extremely busy with life in Atlanta. Malachi and I still talked on the phone occasionally, but it had been months since we had seen each other. I shared my journey in Atlanta, and he seemed to be happy for me. In March 2017, I decided to meet Malachi in L.A. to celebrate his birthday. I needed a vacation.

We were there for three days. During those three days, we partied, hung out with friends, ate at the finest restaurants, went shopping, and enjoyed each other's company. It was beautiful there. We had a blast! This trip allowed us to reconnect, with each other, on a different level. We were still in love with each other. Before we went our separate ways, we promised each other that we would commit to reestablishing our relationship. We agreed to visit each other every month; we would take turns doing so. That is what we did, for the next few months.

Two months later, while visiting Malachi in Ohio, I discovered that I was pregnant. I told Malachi the great news.

While he was getting dressed for a concert, I yelled, "I am pregnant!"

He smiled. I told him that this pregnancy felt differently. I could feel the baby moving inside me.

He responded, "Ok. I am happy for you. Keep me posted!"

He did not say much more about it, so I just changed the subject. He may not have cared, but I did. At my follow-up appointment with Dr. Sam, I heard the baby's heartbeat at 6 weeks and that was the best feeling in the world. I will admit, I was a little nervous at this ultrasound appointment, but within 5 minutes of the ultrasound, she turned the screen around for me to see the baby moving. She also turned the volume up. I just laid there, in total silence and complete disbelief, but happiness. I began to cry. This was the best moment ever, and the first of many heartbeats that I would hear, for the next three years.

Although it was a joyous moment, a part of me was still scared. Afraid. I did not know what to do. I did not know what to expect. I started spotting, lightly, the next few days. However, any time I began to feel nervous that I was losing the baby, Dr. Sam was always there to reassure me that the baby was fine.

I asked, "Am I having a miscarriage?"

"The baby is doing great!" she exclaimed.

"The light bleeding is normal during the first 6-7 weeks of pregnancy; it does not always mean you are having a miscarriage," she continued. "Stop worrying!"

According to Healthline (n.d.), "About 25 percent of pregnant women are estimated to experience spotting during their first 12 weeks of pregnancy. One study from 2010 found that spotting is most commonly seen in the sixth and seventh weeks of pregnancy. Spotting wasn't always a sign of miscarriage or meant that something was wrong."

As time passed, both the baby and I continued to grow. I watched God's magnificent work. A month later, Dr. Sam said that I had to be transferred to a gynecologist for prenatal care. Unfortunately, she did not offer prenatal care services. At my last ultrasound appointment, we heard the baby's heartbeat again, and she provided a list of gynecologists in my area that I could choose from. I was extremely saddened by that news. I found a facility in Decatur, close to the hospital where I would give birth.

Times started to get difficult. I experienced pregnancy alone. The more I shared my medical history, my gynecologists became apprehensive. They were concerned about the risks of me carrying a child. Not only did I have visits at my gynecologist's office, but I was also referred to a maternal-fetal specialist, and had biweekly visits there too. I was a busy mommy-to-be! Due to my age and medical history, I was labeled "high risk" and they treated me as such at every single visit. I was starting to become overwhelmed, so I just started to pray, every chance I could get. I am not bashing my children's father. Everybody's priorities are different, and I respect it, but I wished he could have shared this experience with me.

Chapter 9: Seeing the Light at the end of the Tunnel

He renews my strength. He guides me along the right paths, bringing honor to his name. Even when I walk through the darkest valley, I will not be afraid, for you are close beside me. Your rod and your staff protect and comfort me.

~Psalm 23:3-4

*I*n December 2017, my best friend, Jennifer,

and sorority sister, Bethany, planned a baby

shower for me. I was starting to see the light at

the end of the tunnel. The baby shower was

beautiful. The theme was Prince Charming and

the colors were royal blue and gold. By that

time, I was eight months pregnant. Malachi was

still living in Ohio during my pregnancy, but he

flew into town to attend the baby shower and

the birth of our baby.

Although it was a joyful moment, I did not

feel it. I was humongous. I felt like a pig. On the

day of my baby shower, I reminded myself of my journey to motherhood. That very moment made me appreciate my testimony. I was two weeks away from giving birth to my first child and my mindset changed. I did not care how I looked or felt. I was blessed. I was about to be a mother.

That day, I wore a long, flowing, laced-blue dress. My feet were swollen, so I was happy that my dress covered the slippers on my feet. Many people, including family, friends, and colleagues, showed up to shower my baby with so much love. When I walked down the stairs to greet my family and friends, it felt like heaven. Peace. Love.

Baby Boy was born on January 18, 2018. After years of struggling with miscarriages, I was finally a mother. I can remember that day like it was yesterday. Malachi drove me to the hospital to prepare for my scheduled cesarean section. I was nervous as soon as I walked into the hospital. The night before, I watched a YouTube video that showed a baby being born via cesarean section. I should not have done that.

Are they going to cut me open? Then just pull the baby out? WTH?

As soon as we arrived at the hospital, one of the nurses greeted us at the front entrance and began to introduce herself.

"Hi. My name is Nurse Collins, and I will be assigned to your room today," she asked, 'Are you excited?"

I responded, "I am, but I watched a YouTube video last night of a woman having a c-section. It makes me nervous."

"Do not worry, Ms. Animashaun. The c-section procedure is usually the same process, but every woman's surgery and healing process is different."

"Thank you!" I said nervously.

As soon as she walked us to my assigned room, she handed me a stack of forms to complete, which took me about an hour to do. I rang the nurse's bell to let her know that I was done with the forms and ready to start the preparation process. Ten minutes later, she entered the room and scanned the forms.

"Everything looks good," she exclaimed, 'Let's get you rolled down to the surgery room."

The surgery room was freezing! The doctor entered the room with a huge smile on her face.

"Are you ready, Ms. Animashaun?" she asked.

"Yes, I am," I responded, "but I am a little nervous."

"We are going to take good care of you and the baby," she said excitedly.

"Did someone explain the process to you?" she questioned.

"Yes, I am aware of the process!" I exclaimed.

All of a sudden, it seemed like a thousand doctors were in the room. I am exaggerating, but it had to be at least seven other people in the room, including myself and Malachi. The room was busy. The nurses and doctors were preparing the room with weird-looking instruments and a warmer for the baby. I started to get overwhelmed by the sight, but I glanced over at Malachi, and he just smiled. I was glad that he was there with me. It made me feel a lot better. During preparation, Malachi had to go to the waiting room until surgery began. First, I had to receive an epidural. The epidural would allow me to stay awake and see the birth of my baby while feeling no pain during the surgery. This process took about 20-30 minutes.

"Can you sit up for me please?" the doctor requested.

"Then bend over as if you are reaching for your toes, but not literally," she continued.

It was difficult to see her face in that position, but I began to feel her cold fingers rubbing up and down my spinal cord.

Pressing at a spot on my back, she said, "I am going to stick a needle here."

"It should be a quick shot, please try not to move."

The shot was quick, but it hurt like hell. After about 5 minutes, I was numb. I could not feel anything. Next, I was strapped to the bed, in a T-position, and I saw a catheter placed. The catheter was a thin tube inserted inside my bladder to remove any fluid. This was important during the surgical procedure. I would not be allowed to get up on my own if I needed to use the bathroom. As I lay strapped down to the bed, a white drape was placed above my abdomen, to keep me from seeing directly into the incision (during surgery). However, I could still see the doctors, and most importantly, when the baby was delivered.

Finally, Malachi entered the room with his protective cap and cape on. He sat next to me (near my head), holding my hand firmly, as we waited for the birth of our son. After a few tugs, Baby Boy was born. The doctors held him up in the air, similarly to the scene in the *Lion King* when Simba is held up in the air. I smiled as they laid him on my chest for skin-to-skin. I could not believe that I had a baby. I stayed quiet for a while. Then, they took Baby Boy to clean him and bring him back to my room. I was wheeled to the recovery room. I laid in the hospital bed, for the first time, with pride and happiness. I ended up staying at the hospital for three days, bonding with my baby.

When I was discharged, I called Malachi and told him the great news. He rushed to the hospital, carefully packed the baby and me into the car, and took us home. On the way home, I continued to experience feelings of joy! Although I was in pain from the surgery, I glanced over at the Baby Boy in his car seat and began to cry.

"Are you all right, honey?" Malachi questioned.

"Yes, I am fine," I responded, "I am just happy!"

"We did it!" he exclaimed.

I did not question that statement, but I think he was referring to us finally becoming parents together. A few days later, Malachi flew back to Ohio, and my grandmother came to help with the baby while I still recovered from the surgery. One night, when the meds wore off from having a cesarean section, I cried as I gazed at my baby

221

sleeping peacefully in the bassinet. Then, I grabbed an Ibuprofen and some water from the nightstand, took it, and closed my eyes.

The next year, I watched Baby Boy grow, and it was the best feeling in the world. I never missed a beat. I experienced many firsts with him: teeth, eating baby food or solids, crawling, talking, walking, tantrums, laughing and playing, and so much more. He turned one year old on January 18, 2019. I had survived my first year as a mother.

All year, I had planned an extravagant first birthday party for him. His theme was Boss Baby, and I rented a private room at an indoor play center, called Catch Air. My friend and I arrived about 30 minutes early to decorate the room. He had a Boss Baby-themed birthday cake, cupcakes, and tons of decorations. I had invited almost thirty people to celebrate this special occasion, and surprisingly, they all showed up. He was showered with so much love and gifts! Every time I looked at him, I almost cried. Since becoming a mother, I had transformed into a cry baby! That month, I was in the best place in my life I had ever been.

One day, while thinking about my career, I decided to apply to the Specialist program at Kennesaw State University, and I was accepted! I wanted to pursue my dream that was crushed that traumatic night at Cleveland State University; the night I had my brain hemorrhage. I started graduate school while working and taking care of my son by myself. I wanted my son to be proud of me. I know he will hear my story, later in his life, and appreciate our journey even more.

Additionally, I searched for a neurosurgeon in Atlanta who would accept me as a new neurology patient. It was time that I checked to see if the results of the GKR were successful. It was difficult finding a neurosurgeon because most of them do not prefer to share patients. I truly understand the risks. But, Dr. Roberts accepted me with open arms. I had an MRI scan in October 2018, days after my 35th birthday; and my results were normal. PRAISE GOD!!!

When you are faithful and pray, God always answers your prayers. A month later, I found out I was pregnant again. I was filled with so much happiness. I was not scared as I have been in the past. I knew God was blessing me. I promised myself that I would stay positive throughout my journey, no matter who tried to distract or break me. OH, WHAT A MAGNIFICENT GOD I SERVE!!!!

At 6 weeks, I heard the baby's heartbeat. At 8 weeks, I felt little flutters. At 12 weeks, I felt a kick. At 15 weeks, I found out the sex of the baby. I was having a girl! I wish I could have enjoyed my pregnancy milestones with Baby Boy, but as I mentioned before, I refused to experience another miserable pregnancy. When I found out that my baby was a girl, I immediately shared my great news with my family and friends. They were excited as well and very supportive during my pregnancy; especially my mother. I am just so thankful for all of them.

In addition to my amazing pregnancy news, in April 2019, I became a first-time homeowner.

I spent the summer embracing my unborn baby, continuing to watch my son grow, completing summer graduate courses, and decorating my newly purchased home. God was blessing me, and all I could do was smile. I had two baby showers in October; one at work and my home. We were showered with so much love.

Baby Girl, born on November 1, 2019, was the most beautiful girl I had ever seen. She was astonishing. I always wanted a daughter. I thought about all the fun we would have. The matching outfits. Outings for ice cream. Outings to the hair salon and nail shop. Shopping sprees. Lunch and dinner dates. I also strived to build a better relationship with her than I had with my mother.

On New Year's Eve in 2020, I reflected on my journey. I had two beautiful children. Although I was a single mother raising them, I prayed for them, and I was happy to be their mother. I was happy to be a mother. I prayed for strength and courage. I will forever be grateful and humbled that God blessed me with a second chance. He answered my prayers.

Moreover, I also reflected on my faith. I recognize that he has the final say so. He always makes the final decision. As a result, I finally stopped worrying anymore. Instead, I prayed about everything and stayed positive. Now, I try to be patient and understanding in all situations that I am faced with. It has never failed me. I put forth energy into things and people who are positive and have my best interest at heart. I avoid anything negative, and in this world, I know it is easy to become a victim of it. After my testimony, some people still tried to break me, by attacking me about my past, but what they do not understand is that you cannot break a woman who gets her strength from God. I am that woman. I can no longer be broken.

Chapter 10: Victory

But in your hearts honor Christ the Lord as holy,
always being prepared to make a defense to
anyone who asks you for a reason for the hope
that is in you; yet do it with gentleness and
respect. ~ 1 Peter 3:15

Life was busy, but I was enjoying every moment. A pandemic, COVID-19, stormed the world and changed life forever. I was teaching from home, and at the same time, taking care of the kids. It was rough in the beginning, but like always, I found a way to balance work and home. When my daughter turned four months old, I found out I was pregnant again. Due to the circumstances, I was a little embarrassed because I did not wait a year as the doctors had told me. When I delivered the news to his father, who was newly engaged, I was told to get an abortion. That had to be the dumbest, unsympathetic, and disrespectful thing he could have ever said to me. At 36 years old, I was not ashamed of what I had done, and I was not going to kill an innocent baby.

It is my body! It is my choice.

I did not think twice about having an abortion. I was keeping my baby. I was proud. I had defeated the naysayers. I had defeated the doubters. The victory was mine! After four miscarriages, I was now about to be a mother of three beautiful children. According to Oxford

Learner's Dictionaries (n.d.), victory is defined as "success in a game, an election, a war, etc." The naysayers, doubters, and attackers were the enemy, but God allowed me to defeat them. Successfully giving birth to my children was my victory.

When I shared the good news with family and friends, many of them (who know my journey) jumped for joy, but others began to question my pregnancy.

They questioned, "You're pregnant again? WOW! You did not waste time."

Others asked, "Did you meet another man? Who is the father? Are you ready for three children?"

I felt like screaming. Cursing them out. Instead, I politely told them that it was none of their business. Although I felt like I was being treated like a teen mother, I did not have to share my testimony with people who could not and would not understand it. Moreover, I am a grown-ass woman. I did not have to explain my pregnancy to anyone. I took great care of all my children; I never complained, begged, cried, bothered anyone. My situation would not change with one more child being added to my family. I already knew God was going to take care of us.

I always tried to include family and friends in my children's milestones or memorable events. It was important for my children to be raised in a loving village. Sometimes, people are so bitter, broken, and unhappy with their own lives, that they do not know what to say when you deliver good news to them. They do not know how to be happy for others. I just prayed for them and kept it moving! God blessed me with all my children, and I am grateful. In June 2020, I found I was having a boy! I did not have a preference. Having a healthy child was my priority.

Throughout my pregnancy, again I prayed faithfully. I happily continued to take care of both of my children by myself and completed my last semesters of graduate school. I finished my graduate program that same month. I graduated from Kennesaw State University with a Specialist degree in Instructional Technology.

I hope "the story" behind this degree makes my children proud. Although I did not get to finish my program at Cleveland State University due to my illness, LOOK AT GOD!! I finished another program at another university six years later. I accomplished all of this while being a single mother of two, pregnant, and isolated in my home during the COVID-19 pandemic.

I thank those that took the time to call or text faithfully to check on our well-being, sent money for diapers and wipes, bought clothing (they grow so fast) and learning materials for the children, babysit when I had back-to-back doctor's appointments, went grocery shopping for us, and most importantly, prayed for us. Too many people to name, but THANK YOU!!!!! Papa Smurf was born November 2, 2020, a year and a day after his beautiful big sister! I planned a drive-by birthday party for her, due to the pandemic, and delivered my baby the next day.

Every morning I wake up, I am beyond grateful for my three children. Six years later, victory is mine! This is my testimony.

Blessing #1: Baby Boy

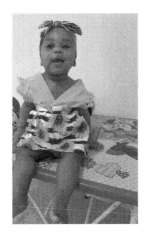

Blessing #2: Baby Girl

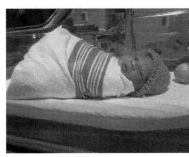

Blessing #3: Papa Smurf

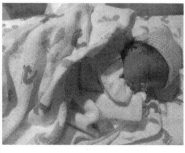

243

"My Greatest Blessings"

Epilogue

Life is too short to worry about anything. Be patient and understanding. This quote has been used regularly in society for centuries. Figuratively speaking, I know that life is short, but how many of us live our lives as if today can be our last? I have experienced several traumatic moments that have shaped my life and caused me to have a more in-depth understanding of these words. Life is too short, which means that our time on earth is not infinite. Something tragic can happen to us, or we can die any day and at any time. In the past, most of my days involved creating a list of "to-do" items and scurrying to complete them by bedtime. Or partying my life away; traveling around the world. I had nothing really valuable to look forward to each day besides work. It was not until I had a near-death experience that made me learn how valuable time, life, family, and friends are.

After my recurrent pregnancy losses, several women would tell me to *trust the process*. Pregnancy and child loss is a very sensitive subject, and it should not be handled like a grain of salt. I never took their advice. I used my faith to heal. I used my therapist to get the strength and courage to break my silence. When I share my story with other women experiencing pregnancy and child loss, I tell them to *trust God*. It may be a cliché statement, but I am a living testimony that when you trust God and are a firm believer, he will answer your prayers. It may not be at the time that you ask, but he always answers them at the right time.

I never discovered the reason I had recurrent miscarriages; sometimes it is unexplainable. But, I know I am not alone. Many women are suffering, in silence, and they do not have to. Pregnancy & Infant Loss Awareness Month was established in 1988 by the United States President Ronald Reagan. He proclaimed that this month would recognize many parents (both mothers and fathers) who had experienced a tragic loss. The recognition was established to show support during such a difficult, yet unique time, of grief. It is mentally, physically, and emotionally draining to suffer from pregnancy or child loss.

On this declaration day, President Ronald Reagan said:

"When a child loses his parent, they are called an orphan. When a spouse loses her or his partner, they are called a widow or widower. When parents lose their children, there isn't a word to describe them. This month recognizes the loss so many parents experience across the United States and around the world. It is also meant to inform and provide resources for parents who have lost children due to miscarriage, ectopic pregnancy, molar pregnancy, stillbirths, birth defects, SIDS, and other causes. Now, Therefore, I, Ronald Reagan, President of the United States of America, do hereby proclaim the month of October as Pregnancy and Infant Loss Awareness Month. I call upon the people of the United States to observe this month with appropriate programs, ceremonies, and activities."

Pregnancy and infant loss describe both miscarriage and stillbirth, but they carry different meanings based on the loss that happened. According to the Center for Disease Control and Prevention (2020), "A stillbirth is the death of a baby before or during delivery. Both miscarriage and stillbirth describe pregnancy loss, but they differ according to when the loss occurs. In the United States, a miscarriage is usually defined as loss of a baby before the 20th week of pregnancy, and stillbirth is loss of a baby at 20 weeks of pregnancy and later."

How many babies are stillborn? Research shows that about 1 in 100 (around 20 weeks of pregnancy and later) is affected by stillbirth or miscarriage. Each year in the United States, approximately 24, 0000 babies are stillborn.

After reading these statistics, you never know who has or is experiencing pregnancy and child loss. I struggled silently for many years after my brain hemorrhage and recurrent miscarriages. It is not a subject to joke or even attack anyone about. Unfortunately, I had to deal with that type of treatment during my bereavement, but it only made me a stronger woman. It is abuse. These "mental abusers" claim to be blessed with impure hearts and bad intentions. First, many people have died or been permanently damaged due to aneurysms, strokes, and other brain malfunctions.

Furthermore, several women are sitting at home suffering due to pregnancy and child loss, feeling ashamed and lost. Questioning their ability as women. Questioning God. I have truly been blessed and highly favored by God. It is an honor to be able to share my testimony with others; whether it affects them mentally, emotionally, or spiritually. I will no longer be silenced, ridiculed, or be made to feel inferior by people that are hurting and broken. Power does not come from hurting others. That is a major sign of weakness. True power comes from helping others.

You may ask: *What can be done to prevent pregnancy and child loss?* Nothing. The causes are still unknown. Stillbirth doesn't discriminate; it can happen to families of all races, ethnicities, socioeconomic status, and women of all ages. I was 30 years old when I had my first miscarriage. I was fit. I would only drink socially. I never smoked. I ate healthy most of the time. I mainly worked and went to the gym; that was my weekly routine.

Pregnancy and child loss can happen to anyone! However, there are some suggestions that women can do to increase their possibility of having a healthy pregnancy and baby.

1. Avoid smoking cigarettes or drinking alcohol during your pregnancy. Avoid any drugs…. Period!

2.Attempt to reach and maintain a healthy
   weight before your pregnancy.

3.If you have any underlying health or
   medical concerns, such as diabetes, high
   blood pressure, make sure you talk to your
   doctor about getting it under control.

Visit cdc.gov to learn more about stillbirth in
the United States. There are hundreds of
support groups on both Facebook and Instagram
(IG), and they are always welcoming new
members. Here a few support groups on IG:

Additionally, I want to share some stroke warning signs. Many people do not know they're having or have had a stroke in men and women. The Centers for Disease Control and Prevention (2020) shares signs of stroke in men and women:

- *Sudden **numbness** or weakness in the face, arm, or leg, especially on one side of the body.*
- *Sudden **confusion**, trouble speaking, or difficulty understanding speech.*
- *Sudden **trouble seeing** in one or both eyes.*

- *Sudden **trouble walking**, dizziness, loss of balance, or lack of coordination.*

- *Sudden **severe headache** with no known cause.*

Call 911 if you or someone is experiencing any of these symptoms.

I pray that this book gives you the courage and strength to heal from your pain, whether you are experiencing pregnancy or child loss, stroke, domestic violence, childhood trauma, or any other tragedy in your life. I also hope that it leads you to your victory. Be proud and encouraged to share your story because once you do, you will feel free. You will have your freedom. Thank you for your love and support.

References

Center for Disease Control and Prevention
   (2020). Stroke signs and symptoms. Retrieved
   March 1, 2021, from
   https://www.cdc.gov/stroke/signs_symptoms.htm

Center for Disease Control and Prevention
   (2020). Pregnancy and infant loss.
   Retrieved March 1, 2021, from
   https://www.cdc.gov/ncbddd/stillbirth/features/pregna
   ncy-infant-loss.html

Oxford Learner's Dictionary (n.d.). Victory. In
   OxfordLearnersDictionaries.com.
   Retrieved January 5, 2021, from
   https://www.oxfordlearnersdictionaries.com/us/defini
   tion/american_english/victory#:~:text=noun-,noun,el
   ection%2C%20a%20war%2C%20etc

About the Author

SIMBI M. ANIMASHAUN is currently a middle school English teacher in Decatur, GA. She has over ten years in the educational system. She enjoys teaching, reading, writing, and spending quality time with her three children. Her love for children drives her to open her school or daycare one day. She has sponsored many programs for children, such as the step team, National Junior Beta Club, and an annual girl's conference that focused on several topics affecting girls between the ages of 10-14.

Simbi's highest level of education is a Specialist degree in Instructional Technology, which was earned from Kennesaw State University. She is also a member of Alpha Kappa Alpha Sorority, Inc. To conclude, Simbi aspires to be a motivational speaker with a focus on healing and empowerment amid pregnancy and child loss. Moreover, she is currently designing a workshop, *The Power of Healing*, and a workbook to accompany it. Moreover,

Simbi is open about sharing her story of pregnancy loss with others. Her social media platform regularly addresses her struggle with pregnancy loss. She is a member of many support groups, both formally and informally.